Stories of *Titanic's* SECOND CLASS

BY RACHEL A. BAILEY

The Child's World®
childsworld.com

Published by The Child's World®
1980 Lookout Drive • Mankato, MN 56003-1705
800-599-READ • www.childsworld.com

Acknowledgments
The Child's World®: Mary Berendes, Publishing Director
Red Line Editorial: Design, editorial direction, and production
Photographs ©: Bain Collection/Library of Congress, cover, 1, 15, 19; PA Wire/AP
Images, 4; Library of Congress, 6; The Mariners' Museum/Corbis, 8; Harris & Ewing/
Library of Congress, 11; Ralph White/Corbis, 12; Daily Mirror/Mirrorpix/Corbis, 16;
Bettmann/Corbis, 20

ISBN 9781634074674

LCCN 2015946305

Printed in the United States of America
Mankato, MN
December, 2015
PA02287

ABOUT THE AUTHOR

Rachel A. Bailey grew up in a small Kansas town. As a child, she enjoyed
reading and taking walks in the forest with her Australian shepherd dog.
Bailey is a former gifted education teacher. She now writes children's
magazine articles and curriculum for teachers. This is her fourth book.

Table of
CONTENTS

Launch

OF

White Star Royal Mail Triple-Screw Steamer

"TITANIC"

At BELFAST,

Wednesday, 31st May, 1911, at 12-15 p.m.

Admit Bearer.

Chapter 1

UNSINKABLE

On April 10, 1912, people crowded excitedly around a dock in Southampton, England. They watched as passengers boarded a massive, beautiful ship. The *Titanic* was the largest ship in the world. It was filled with fine rooms and furnishings. People also believed that it was sturdy and safe. *Shipbuilder* magazine said the boat was "practically unsinkable."[1]

Lawrence Beesley was a science teacher in England. He planned to sail on the *Titanic* to the United States. He would tour New York and then visit his brother in Canada. Beesley bought a second-class ticket for the journey. He paid 12 **pounds** for his ticket. That's the same as $1,375 for a ticket today. First-class passengers paid even more for their tickets. Some spent up to $100,000 in today's money. The cheapest ticket on the *Titanic* was for third class. It cost $350 in today's money.

Beesley's ticket was expensive, but he knew it was worth the price. He was excited to travel on the largest ship of all time. Beesley's friends came to say good-bye before his adventure. He explored the second-class decks, dining salons, and library. There was even an elevator for the passengers. A gymnasium allowed them to exercise while at sea. Second-class rooms were large, with fine, comfortable furnishings. They were similar to first-class areas on other boats. The first-class rooms on the *Titanic* were even more **luxurious**. Beesley declared that "it was quite easy to lose one's way on such a ship."[2]

Other second-class passengers were also exploring the ship. Edward and Ethel Beane had just celebrated their wedding in England. Edward had found work as a bricklayer in the United

▲ **The second-class quarters contained passengers traveling alone as well as children and families.**

States. The Beanes were traveling to their new home in New York. They brought $500 and their 65 wedding gifts on the ship with them.

Edwina "Winnie" Troutt was 27 years old when she boarded the *Titanic*. Her sister was having a baby. Troutt was traveling to the United States to help her. Troutt shared a **cabin** on Deck E with two other women. The cabin included two bunk beds and a washbasin.

One of Troutt's roommates, Nora Keane, worried about the safety of the ship. She did not believe it was unsinkable. She fretted, "I should never be on this ship. It will never reach New York!"[3] But others were excited to set sail.

Shortly after noon, the ship's whistles blew. The noise signaled the start of the *Titanic*'s voyage. The grand ship would make stops in France and Ireland. Then it would **embark** on the journey across the Atlantic Ocean. New York would be the ship's last stop.

For the first few days of the journey, the sea was calm. First-class and second-class passengers enjoyed watching the scenery on the upper Boat Deck. Troutt made new friends and played cards. The Beanes spent evenings talking with other passengers in the second-class lounge. Beesley spent much of his time on the outside decks. He enjoyed the brisk air. But on Sunday, April 14, Beesley moved inside. The temperature outside had dropped quickly. The ship was heading for icy waters.

Chapter 2

ICY DANGERS

After a few days at sea, Lawrence Beesley was relaxing in the dining saloon. On the evening of April 14, a crowd gathered and began to sing songs. Some were old sailing songs, such as "For Those in Peril on the Sea." These songs described shipwrecks and other dangers. But most passengers on the *Titanic* felt safe. Few noticed signs of danger.

The singing lasted until about 10:00 p.m. Then the **stewards** served biscuits and coffee. Second-class passengers lingered in the saloon talking. At 10:45 p.m., Beesley retired to his cabin. It was three floors below the Boat Deck. The Boat Deck was on the top of the ship.

Beesley put on pajamas and prepared to sleep. He settled into his bed to read. At around 11:45 p.m., he felt his mattress vibrating. With a jolt, the ship stopped moving. He put on his robe and went up to the Boat Deck.

The air was icy on the deck. Beesley saw people talking, but none of them seemed concerned. They did not know why the boat had stopped. Beesley wandered to the second-class lounge. A man there had spotted a large iceberg. It was about 80 feet (24 m) tall. Beesley grew worried. Had the ship hit the iceberg? But then the ship started moving again. Beesley returned to his cabin. He comforted himself by reading.

A loud noise distracted him from his book. Then a man shouted, "All passengers on deck with lifebelts on!"[4] Beesley threw on his jacket and trousers. He put his book in his pocket and headed back up to the top deck. Beesley's fears had come true. The ship had hit a large iceberg.

Beesley was not the only passenger on edge. Earlier that evening, Winnie Troutt had also watched the community singing. At 10:30 p.m., she began to feel chilly. Troutt returned to her room to sleep. But she woke at 11:40 p.m. when she felt the ship jolt. Worried, she walked up to the second-class lounge.

"What's the matter with the boat?" she asked.

"Oh, it isn't anything," a man responded. "We just grazed an iceberg."[5]

Troutt rushed back down to her cabin. She woke her two roommates and told them about the iceberg. The women dressed quickly and sprinted to the Boat Deck.

Edward and Ethel Beane slept through the ship's **collision** with the iceberg. Noise from the halls finally woke them. Passengers were talking about lifeboats. But the Beanes thought they were just missing a boat **drill**. Finally, a woman in the cabin next to them insisted that they go upstairs. The Beanes left their jewels and other beautiful wedding gifts behind. When they reached the Boat Deck, they realized the trouble they were in. Officers were preparing passengers to board lifeboats.

Passengers on the Boat Deck bundled up in coats and shawls. They waited for orders from the crew. Most waited calmly. They talked and listened to music from the ship's band. But the passengers were nervous about possible dangers. They did not

▲ Stewards on the *Titanic*, photographed after the sinking, had the task of helping passengers.

know it yet, but the iceberg had ripped the ship's **hull**. Water poured in, filling the lower decks of the massive ship. The *Titanic* was not unsinkable. The ship was doomed.

Chapter 3

ESCAPING THE SHIP

The ship soon began to lean to one side. Passengers were frantic. At 12:20 a.m., bright lights burst upward. "Rockets!" some shouted. The rockets were a distress signal. The *Titanic*'s crew hoped people on nearby ships would see them. The ships could rescue the *Titanic* passengers.

Suddenly, a ship officer appeared. "All women and children get down to the deck below!" he yelled. "All men stand back from the boats."[6]

Crew members began to help women and children into lifeboats. Edward Beane watched his wife, Ethel, board Lifeboat #13. He promised that he would see her soon.

Winnie Troutt's two roommates immediately boarded a lifeboat. While Troutt stood nearby, a frantic man thrust a baby into her arms. He could not find the baby's mother. The man was not allowed to go into a lifeboat himself. Troutt brought the baby with her into Lifeboat #16. She agreed to look after the child. All she carried was a toothbrush, a book, and the baby.

Soon, crew members launched the lifeboats on the **starboard** side of the top deck. Most of the second-class women and children made it into the boats. But hundreds of men in second class still needed rescue. Many walked to the **port** side of the ship. They hoped to find lifeboats there. Most were out of luck. The *Titanic* did not have enough lifeboats for all its passengers.

Beesley stayed on the starboard side and waited. He looked over the edge of the ship. Soon, he spotted a crew member standing in Lifeboat #13. The lifeboat was suspended from ropes. It still had room for more people.

The crew member asked, "Any ladies on your deck?"

"No," Beesley answered.

"Then you had better jump," said the crew member.[7] Beesley sat on the edge of the deck and dangled his feet. He held his breath and jumped.

Beesley landed with a thud in Lifeboat #13. He helped a crew member push the boat away from the sinking *Titanic*. The two men worked to cut the ropes. Meanwhile, Edward was still watching the lifeboat. His wife, Ethel, was inside. He waited for Lifeboat #13 to land safely in the water. Then Edward leapt into the water and swam to the boat. Ethel used all her strength to pull him in.

From Lifeboat #16, Winnie Troutt heard the band playing songs as the ship slowly sank. The lights on the *Titanic* flickered and then went out. The **bow** tilted downward. Water began to cover the lowest row of porthole windows. By 2:00 a.m., the water completely covered the bow. The ship's machine parts roared as they were torn from the ship. Beesley described the sound as a "rattle and a groaning that could be heard for miles."[8]

More than 1,000 passengers were still on the ship. They wailed as they jumped into the icy water. Their cries haunted the

▲ **Early on April 15, 1912, *Titanic*
survivors spied the RMS *Carpathia*.**

passengers in Lifeboat #13. Finally, the large vessel disappeared under the water. A crew member on the lifeboat ordered the passengers to row away from the people in the water. They did not have the space for more survivors. Overcrowding the lifeboats might cause them to sink.

The lifeboat passengers rowed in the dark, shivering in shawls and blankets. They scanned the water for light from a ship. For hours, they searched and waited. Suddenly, a light appeared in the distance. It grew brighter and brighter. It was a large ship coming their way. At 4:00 a.m., the RMS *Carpathia* reached Lifeboat #13.

Chapter 4

THE RESCUE

Crew members on the *Carpathia* brought up passengers from one lifeboat at a time. At 8:30 a.m., all of the *Titanic* survivors were on board. Many were exhausted from hours of rowing the lifeboats. Still, they were lucky to be alive. Only 706 passengers of the *Titanic* survived. The remaining 1,517 passengers died at sea.

Most women and children in second class survived the sinking. But most men did not. There had been 168 men traveling in second class. Only 14 were saved. That was less than the number of first-class or third-class men who survived. Many second-class men had difficulty finding lifeboats with enough space.

On the *Carpathia*, crew members gave the survivors coats and hot tea. Many survivors had only the clothes on their backs. Some second-class passengers wore formal gowns. Others were in their nightclothes.

Survivors stayed in the saloons and library. Many slept on tables or in corners. Lawrence Beesley made a bed out of towels on the bathroom floor. Space was limited. The best places went to first-class passengers.

Winnie Troutt arrived on the *Carpathia* with the baby she had cared for. Luckily, the mother spotted her child. The two were reunited. Troutt slept the first night on a table. But the next night, she became upset by a severe storm. Troutt worried that the *Carpathia* was also headed for disaster. Someone found her a bed to sleep in, which calmed her.

The *Carpathia* sailed for three days after the *Titanic* sank. On April 18, the ship landed safely in New York City. Thousands of Americans waited for the passengers. People cried and hugged the survivors. Bells tolled to honor the *Titanic* passengers who died.

Survivors remembered the disaster in different ways. Beesley wrote a book about his experience. *The Loss of the S.S. Titanic* was published two months after the ship sank. The book became popular. Readers wanted to know what it was like to survive the disaster. But Beesley was still haunted by his experience. He never traveled on a ship again.

Ethel and Edward Beane lost everything when the *Titanic* sank. Their 65 wedding gifts went down with the ship. They also lost their life savings. Yet they still had each other.

At first, the Beanes refused to speak publicly about the disaster. The sinking was a painful memory. They only shared their story with family members. "For years I didn't want to talk about it," Ethel said. "Wherever we went, people pointed at us curiously, and made us aware that death had brushed us by."[9] Finally, Ethel decided that their story was important. She shared it with others in letters and interviews.

Second-class passenger Stuart Collett, a minister, was ▶ photographed on the *Carpathia*.

Winnie Troutt (later Winnie Mackenzie) also mourned the loss of the *Titanic*. She often thought about the people who died. Years later, Troutt still thought of the ship every day. She said, "I have vivid dreams of the *Titanic* and every time I see the ship she's way up in the sky, which I don't understand. I see the *Titanic* full blast always up in the sky, but I've never dreamed of her going down or anything. I've never had any nasty dreams about her."[10]

Troutt lived to be 100 years old. Despite her sadness about the *Titanic*, she continued to travel on ships. By the time she died, she had crossed the Atlantic Ocean more than 10 times. Troutt often spoke about her memories of the *Titanic*. She wanted everyone to remember what happened on the ship. Like the Beanes, she knew she had an important story to tell.

◀ **In 1977, Winnie Mackenzie (formerly Winnie Troutt) looked at a model of the *Titanic* in Los Angeles, California.**

GLOSSARY

bow (BO): The bow is the front part of a ship or boat. The bow of the *Titanic* was the first part to sink.

cabin (KA-bin): A cabin is a room where passengers stay and sleep on a ship. Some passengers on the *Titanic* shared a cabin.

collision (kuh-LI-zhuhn): A collision is a bump or crash. A collision with an iceberg caused the *Titanic* to sink.

drill (DRIL): A drill is a way for people to practice a skill or activity. The ship officers had a drill to practice how to act in an emergency.

embark (em-BARK): To embark is to begin a journey or set sail. The *Titanic* would embark from Southampton, England.

hull (HUHL): The hull is the rigid frame and outer shell of a ship. The hull of the *Titanic* scraped against an iceberg.

luxurious (luk-SHUH-ree-us): When something is luxurious, it is very fine or expensive. Passengers loved the luxurious cabins.

port (PORT): The port side is the left side when one is facing the front of a ship from the inside. The lifeboat was held on the port side of the ship.

pounds (POUNDZ): Pounds are a type of money from Britain. A second-class ticket on the *Titanic* cost 12 pounds.

starboard (STAHR-bord): The starboard side is the right side when one is facing the front of a ship from the inside. Some lifeboats were held on the starboard side of the ship.

stewards (STOO-erds): Stewards are helpers who take care of the passengers on ships. The stewards guided passengers to the lifeboats.

SOURCE NOTES

1. Andrew Wilson. *Shadow of the Titanic: The Extraordinary Stories of Those Who Survived.* New York: Atria, 2012. Print. 18.

2. Lawrence Beesley. *The Loss of the S.S. Titanic.* Project Gutenberg, 16 Mar. 2014. Web. 16 May 2015.

3. Steve McMillian. "Titanic Survivor Speaks in 1974 Interview about the Shipwreck." *Denver Post.* Digital First Media, 27 April 2012. Web. 31 May 2015.

4. Lawrence Beesley. *The Loss of the S.S. Titanic.* Project Gutenberg, 16 Mar. 2014. Web. 16 May 2015.

5. Ibid.

6. Ibid.

7. Ibid.

8. Lawrence Beesley. "Titanic Stood on End for Minutes Before She Sunk." *Encyclopedia Titanica.* Encyclopedia Titanica, 2005. Web. 16 May 2015.

9. Margaret Frawley. "Sinking of Titanic Still Horror to Couple Honeymooning on Ship." *Encyclopedia Titanica.* Encyclopedia Titanica, 28 Aug. 2003. Web. 13 May 2015.

10. Steve Futterman and Edwina MacKenzie. "Edwina MacKenzie." *BBC Archives.* BBC, n.d. Web. 1 June 2015.

TO LEARN MORE

Books

Denenberg, Barry. *Titanic Sinks!* New York: Viking, 2011.

Hopkinson, Deborah. *Titanic: Voices from the Disaster.* New York: Scholastic, 2012.

Stewart, David. *You Wouldn't Want to Sail on the Titanic! One Voyage You'd Rather Not Make.* Danbury, CT: Franklin Watts, 2013.

Web Sites

Visit our Web site for links about the *Titanic*'s second class:
childsworld.com/links

Note to Parents, Teachers, and Librarians: We routinely verify our Web links to make sure they are safe and active sites. So encourage your readers to check them out!

INDEX